Business Storytelling
Harnessing Communication for Strategic Growth

Table of Contents

Chapter 1. Introduction

Unlock the power of narratives in business with this Special Report on "Business Storytelling: Harnessing Communication for Strategic Growth." This is not another cookie-cutter business manual. Prepare yourself for an inspiring journey through the untapped possibilities of storytelling crafted for corporate professionals just like you. Learn how the magic of human connection inherent in narratives can become a game-changing tool in your strategic arsenal. We guarantee that no reader will remain untouched by the rich insight this life-altering report offers. Investing in this report is not just a purchase; it's the next step in your journey towards top-tier communication, strategic growth, and achieving your business aspirations. And remember, your story is where your success begins!

Chapter 2. The Art and Science of Business Storytelling

Storytelling is often perceived as an art, a creative endeavor limited to writers, artists, and filmmakers. Yet, it is essentially a human skill that has been vital to our survival as a species. It has facilitated the sharing of knowledge and wisdom, cultivated empathy, and nurtured communities since the dawn of civilization. Today, businesses can harness the power of storytelling to bridge gaps, inspire change, boost performance, and create compelling visions for the future. What follows is an exploration into the art and science of business storytelling—its elements, significance, tactics, and tips for mastery.

2.1. Unveiling the Concept

Business storytelling is the process of crafting persuasive, relatable, and engaging narratives that communicate a company's vision, mission, or core values to its stakeholders—employees, customers, investors, and the broader community. It's an inspiring and persuasive communication strategy that fosters trust, nurtures relationships, and compels action.

Stories create meaningful experiences. They possess the power to transform dry, statistical data into engaging, memorable content influencing behavior and decision-making. In a business context, storytelling is not about concocting tales but about assembling truths in a manner that speaks to the human heart. It's about sparking an emotional response that influences perceptions, attitudes, and actions beneficial to the business.

2.2. The Power of Narratives in Business

The human brain is wired for stories. We naturally seek patterns and connections, and we derive meaning from them. Narratives harness this propensity, captivating attention, and fostering empathy.

Business narratives are impactful for several reasons:

- They humanize brands: Stories infuse personality into otherwise impersonal corporations, creating emotional connections with stakeholders and setting the company apart from competitors.

- Simplify complex information: Illustrating complicated ideas or data through storytelling makes them more digestible and memorable.

- Stimulate action: Well-crafted business narratives inspire employees, convince investors, and sway customers, compelling them to take desired actions.

2.3. Bridging the Gap between Art and Science

The art of storytelling revolves around crafting engaging, persuasive narratives, using human experiences and emotions as its primary tools. The science, on the other hand, employs neurology and psychology, incorporating the knowledge of how our brains respond to stories.

The art in business storytelling lies in its creative execution. An effective business story is short yet profound, personal yet universal, factual yet emotive. It stays true to the brand while resonating with its audience.

The science lies in understanding the audience's psyche. It requires insight into the behaviors, needs, and aspirations of the target audience. Knowing what triggers emotions, empathy, or actions in your audience would guide the crafting and delivery of effective business narratives.

2.4. Elements of an Effective Business Story

All compelling stories, including business narratives, contain certain pivotal elements:

- A relatable hero (the protagonist)
- Challenges or conflicts that the hero must overcome (the plot)
- A resolution, showing how the hero surmounts these challenges

In a corporate setting, your brand, product, or services, or the audience itself could be portrayed as the hero. The conflict could focus on marketplace challenges, customer pain points, or internal hurdles. The resolution should always exhibit how your brand or solution aids in overcoming these problems.

2.5. Crafting Your Business Narrative

Creating a potent business story demands a deep understanding of your brand, audience, and objectives. These steps can guide your narrative creation:

- Identify Your Story: Discover the narratives embedded in your brand identity, customer experiences, employee testimonials, or company culture.
- Know Your Audience: Define who your audience is, what they

care about, what motivates them, and how they perceive your brand.

- Define Your Objectives: Determine what action you want your audience to take after hearing or reading your story.

- Construct the Arc: Create a powerful beginning (set the context), middle (infuse conflict), and end (provide resolution).

- Stir Emotions: People remember what they feel more than what they know. Invoke emotion to make your messages stick—they could be joy, surprise, trust, or even calculated touches of fear or sadness.

- Keep it Authentic: Authenticity reinforces credibility. Avoid embellishing facts or making false claims.

- Call to Action: Encourage your audience to act in alignment with your determined objectives.

2.6. Tips for Masterful Narration

Masterful storytelling isn't an overnight task—it necessitates practice and patience. Here are some tips to hone your art:

- Use vivid and sensory language to invoke imagination.

- Show, don't just tell—leverage the audience's senses to paint a picture, rather than only stating facts.

- Engage your audience—interactivity boosts engagement and memorability. Let your audience participate in your story. Pose questions, invite opinions, or create interactive content.

- Foster empathy—build narratives around real people dealing with real issues. Demonstrating understanding and empathy can help to build long-lasting bonds with your audience.

- Rely on consistency—maintaining a consistent narrative across multiple platforms reinforces your brand's identity and message, especially in the digital age.

In conclusion, the art and science of business storytelling interweave seamlessly to create an influential communication strategy that can drive change, inspire performance, and shape a compelling vision. It's all about curating and sharing stories that align with your brand's ethos and your audience's expectations, transforming the mundane into the memorable. Embarking on the journey of business storytelling not only enhances business communication but also lends impetus to strategic growth. After all, every business has a story to tell; the key to success lies in telling it well.

Chapter 3. Understanding the Power of Story in Corporate Communication

The corporate world has long been depicted as a dry, unemotional space dominated by data analysis and scientific decision-making. Of course, data is essential, statistics are crucial, but is there something we are missing? Absolutely! That's storytelling, a potent tool, often grievously overlooked, which can take your company's communication from mundane to mesmerizing.

3.1. The Philosophy of Storytelling

Much of the power of business storytelling lies in its ability to bridge the gap between facts and emotions. The human mind tends to retain experience much more effectively than raw data. A well-crafted story fulfils this need by making data relatable and memorable. Albert Einstein, a great scientist who understood the power of narrative, summed it up: "If you can't explain it simply, you don't understand it well enough."

Storytelling, essentially, is the art of narrating events in a structured and interactive way, having a plot, characters, and a resolution—a close reflection of our lives. The same principle applies to business storytelling. The business represents the 'character,' while its journey constitutes the 'plot.'

3.2. The Science behind Storytelling

You might question, "Do people really remember stories better than data?" The answer is yes, and there's scientific evidence to back it up. Stories impact the brain in ways that data cannot. They ignite the region related to sensing and motor skills, making listeners feel as though they're a part of the story. They stimulate neurotransmitters like dopamine and oxytocin, which are related to memory formation and empathy, respectively. So, the next time you want your colleagues to remember a crucial point, try packing it in a powerful narrative.

3.3. Storytelling: A Catalyst for Corporate Communication

Storytelling can provide much-needed glue to bind all the elements of corporate communication. It can shape a brand, sell a strategy, build a culture, or even drive change.

1. Brand Identity: Customers don't invest in products or services; they invest in a brand's story that resonates with their values. A brand story imbued with a purpose helps build trust and loyalty.

2. Strategy Sharing: Instead of presenting bullet points of a new strategy, narrate a story of how it was conceived, the problem it addresses, and the envisioned future.

3. Building Culture: Stories can exemplify a company's values, tradition, and culture vividly, fostering a sense of identity among employees. To nurture an innovative culture, share stories of triumphs arising from innovation.

4. Driving Change: Resistance to change is rooted in fear and uncertainty. Storytelling can paint a picture of a positive future derived from change, helping to drive transformation.

3.4. Translating Facts into Stories

It's crucial to understand how to translate fact into narrative. Begin by identifying the essential pieces of your story - the character, the challenge, the journey, and the resolution.

Once done, craft your story, keeping it simple yet appealing. Use a conversational tone to make it relatable. Maintain a consistent flow to ensure the audience does not lose interest. And lastly, align it to the 'character' — your brand, your strategy, or your culture.

3.5. The Power in Vulnerability

Some of the finest business stories come from vulnerability and overcoming the odds. It could be early failures, financial struggles, or a tough market penetration. Sharing these stories makes the company appear authentic and humanizes the brand, driving a stronger emotional connection.

3.6. Using Stories for Stakeholder Engagement

Stakeholders are essential to a corporate's survival and success. Communicating business strategy, corporate governance, sustainability practices, and more can be made impactful through stories. The key lies in tailoring these narratives to the stakeholder's perspective, demonstrating the value it offers to them.

Taking a strategic leap into the power of storytelling can revolutionize corporate communication. While data drives decisions, stories drive action. Start using narratives as a strategic tool, and watch as it transforms the way you connect, communicate, and convince in the corporate world. It's time to harness the emotional power of storytelling and combine it with the logical prowess of data and analysis, ascend into a new era of effective corporate communication.

Chapter 4. The Psychology of Storytelling: Creating Emotional Resonance

Storytelling has been a potent tool in human communication since time immemorial. The art of molding experiences, feelings, and lessons into compelling narratives is far from a recent discovery. Rather, it is an intrinsic human instinct - one that has shaped societies, traditions, and yes, even businesses.

In today's corporate world, storytelling is becoming an integral aspect of effective communication and strategic growth. But why is that? What makes storytelling such an influential force? It boils down to one fundamental factor - the human brain's unique response to stories.

=== Neuroscience Behind the Attraction to Storytelling

Scientifically, our penchant for stories is deeply rooted in neuroscience. Stories engage our brains differently than raw data or pure information. When you read or hear a list of facts, only the language processing part of your brain gets activated to decode the meaning. In contrast, a story activates several parts of the brain - the ones that would be used if you were living the event yourself.

This experience, known as neural coupling, allows listeners to turn the story into their own ideas and experiences, leading to better understanding and recall. More interestingly, a well-told story can even sync the brain activity of the storyteller and listener, a process known as neural entrainment. This unifying power of storytelling fosters empathy, trust, and connection - qualities indispensable in the world of business.

=== Emotion: The Heart of Effective Storytelling

What makes a narrative more engaging than a list of data points? Emotions. Emotionally charged events are more easily remembered than neutral ones, and it is precisely this principle that makes storytelling a formidable tool.

This phenomenon is called the Amygdala Effect, named after a part of the brain that processes emotional responses. The amygdala stimulates the release of dopamine, a neurotransmitter that helps regulate the brain's reward and pleasure centers, enhancing our memory and information processing.

In a business setting, eliciting emotions through storytelling can effectively connect with stakeholders, influence decision-making, and build brand loyalty.

=== Creating Emotional Resonance through Stories

So how can one create an emotionally resonant story? There are numerous elements, from language and structure to content and context. However, the following key points have proven particularly effective.

1. **Authenticity**: The most emotionally resonant stories are those that come from a place of sincerity. Authenticity breeds trust and creates a layer of credibility that is difficult to replicate.

2. **Relatability**: Engaging stories are usually ones that the reader or listener can identify with on some level. A relatable dilemma or a common experience can strike a chord, and the more people identify with the narrative, the stronger its influence.

3. **Conflict and Resolution**: A compelling story takes the reader on a journey, ideally through conflicts and towards a satisfying resolution. The struggle creates tension, engages the reader's emotions, and the eventual triumph provides relief, satisfaction, and motivation.

4. **Visual Imagery**: Using evocative language to create vivid mental

images can engage the reader's emotions and memories, increasing empathy and connection.

=== Utilizing the Power of Metaphors

Metaphors are the secret ingredient to making your business narrative irresistible. They suggest a similarity between two concepts, making complex ideas more digestible and memorable. When used correctly, metaphors can evoke emotions, create strong mental images, and reinforce your message.

For example, you might say, "Our company navigated the stormy seas of the recession," instead of simply stating, "We survived the recession." The metaphor paints a more vibrant picture, underscoring the struggles endured and victories achieved.

=== Storytelling and Empathy: A Pathway to Connection

Empathy, the ability to understand and share the feelings of others, is central to the impact of storytelling. Stories can help us step into another's shoes, see things from a different perspective, and connect on a deep, emotional level.

When this is employed effectively in a business context, it can deepen relationships with customers, employees, or investors. A CEO who shares his personal journey, a brand that tells the story of its origin, or a salesperson who uses a client's success story to illustrate the benefits of a product - they all generate empathy and form a visceral connection.

In summary, understanding the psychological aspects of storytelling enables us to craft powerful narratives that drive emotional resonance. Rich in emotion and authenticity, stories have the power to foster connections, influence decisions, and promote strategic growth. After all, at the heart of every successful business is a compelling story – one that resonates, inspires, and propels the brand towards its lofty aspirations.

Chapter 5. Crafting Your Company's Narrative: Where to Start

A compelling narrative can be the key to connect with your stakeholders in powerful ways. It shares your company's aspirations and challenges, forms a bridge between your brand and customers, and leverages the raw power of stories in shaping human sentiment and behaviour. Crafting your company's narrative, however, is an art that calls for clarity, creativity, and a deep understanding of your company's core. In the following pages, we'll go through the step by step process of creating a narrative that resonates and serves as the bedrock of your business arsenal.

5.1. Begin with the End in Mind

As with any story, understanding where you want your narrative to lead is crucial for charting your journey. Begin by clearly defining the goal of your company's narrative. Are you aiming for increased brand awareness, forging stronger customer relationships, or perhaps internal alignment within the organization? Clarify the heart of your narrative and ensure it aligns with the overarching business vision and strategic objectives.

Next, identify your audience. Knowing who your story is supposed to reach is equally as important as the story itself. Be clear about your stakeholders - these could be your customers, employees, investors, partners, or even broader society. Understanding their needs, aspirations, and challenges will fine-tune your narrative to resonate and make an impact.

In this first step, there's no need for elaborate detail, just clear intent and a broad direction. It's the foundation upon which we'll build the subsequent elements of your narrative.

5.2. Crafting the Core Message

Every captivating narrative has a potent central theme. Apple's core message, for instance, revolves around 'innovation and simplicity,' which permeates across their products, services, marketing, and every stratum of their business. Your core message is the essence of your narrative used to communicate your mission and vision.

Remember that your core message is not a product pitch, service description, or business model. Think broadly about the values your company espouses, the broader purpose you serve in your market, and the distinctive essence that sets you apart. This pivotal point is from where the strands of your narrative will start weaving.

5.3. Harness the Power of Authenticity

Transparency and authenticity play a vital role in today's business narratives. The days of hiding behind polished business fronts are long gone, replaced by a societal desire for authentic and transparent business practices. Your narrative should incorporate the highs and lows, the successes and failures, and the effort behind your growth. Share the real human stories within your organization, showing your audience that your business is composed of people working tirelessly to provide them with value.

Importantly, maintain consistency in your narrative. Consistency is key in all aspects of your story, from the tone and language, to the themes and messages. Inconsistencies can confuse your audience and dilute your message.

5.4. Leveraging Storytelling Techniques

Good storytelling can transform a mundane fact-filled narration into an engaging tale. Plot development, character creation, the use of suspense, and a climactic conclusion are all tools at your disposal.

For business narratives, your company is the main character, with objectives (your mission), challenges (market competition, internal roadblocks etc.), and transformative moments (breakthrough products, services etc.). You can talk about your company's humble beginnings, its struggles, and its triumphant moments. But remember, the focus should remain on how your company delivers value to its audience.

5.5. Evolving Narratives

The narrative of your company is not a static construct, but a dynamic and evolving entity. It will grow and develop as your business navigates the unpredictable and tumultuous waves of the market. Therefore, it's integral to revisit and revise your narrative consistently to reflect the current stage and aspirations of your company. Allow it to breathe, mature, and evolve.

In conclusion, a well-crafted narrative can be a transformative tool in your business arsenal. It tightly weaves your company's essence, vision, and mission into a compelling storyline that resonates with your audience on a human level. By following the steps outlined above, you can start the journey of crafting your company's narrative, shaping profound connections, driving strategic growth, and articulating your unique value proposition to the world. The magic of narrative awaits, and with it, a world of untapped possibilities.

Chapter 6. Strategic Storytelling: Frameworks and Techniques

When enterprises venture into the realm of business storytelling, their success heavily depends on understanding and implementing certain strategies, frameworks, and techniques. Storytelling can shape and mold brand power, stir emotions, and encourage action in ways that numbers and statistics cannot. The power of business storytelling not only enhances customer engagement but also fosters innovation, enhances organizational culture, and redefines leadership styles. In this chapter, we delve into the powerful world of strategic storytelling, discussing various frameworks and techniques that serve to amplify the impact.

6.1. Understanding Strategic Storytelling

Strategic storytelling is a planned, deliberate act, designed to bring you closer to achieving your business goals. It has a particular structure and purpose, targeting specific audiences. More than just a narrative, it is about using storytelling for business growth. It is choosing the right story in the right context, told in the right manner, and to the right audience.

The concept of strategic storytelling isn't a new one. It traces back to ancient history where tribes used stories to pass down the wisdom of how to hunt, cook, and survive. Similarly, businesses utilize strategic storytelling to convey their values, establish their brand persona, build relationships with consumers, convey their mission, or inspire organizational culture.

6.2. The Frameworks of Strategic Storytelling

Numerous frameworks can guide you in the process of creating your strategic story. These frameworks not only help you to shape your story but also make sure it resonates with your intended audience.

1. **Hero's Journey**: This narrative structure is utilized in various mediums and is universally understood and appreciated. The protagonist confronts a challenge, fails, learns, and finally overcomes adversity, often transforming in the process. For businesses, these stories can resonate deeply with audiences as they reflect human experiences of failure, resilience, and transformation.

2. **Three-Act Structure**: This is a familiar storytelling structure for both movies and novels often described as 'Setup-Conflict-Resolution.' In a business context, this could be set up as 'Problem-Solution-Benefit.'

3. **Mountain**: This narrative structure reveals a situation, introduces problems or complications, gradually builds up to a climax, and finally ends with a resolution.

4. **Nested Loops**: This involves a series of three or more narratives that are interconnected in some way where each story leads to the next. The end of the last narrative takes the audience back to the first narrative.

Remember, it is not only about choosing a specific framework but also ensuring that you are crafting a story that aligns with your business context and objectives.

6.3. Techniques for Effective Business Storytelling

After you have chosen your framework, you need to employ various storytelling techniques to ensure that your story is compelling and impactful. Here are some techniques that work particularly well:

1. **Visual Stimulation**: Utilize the vivid details in your story to paint a picture in the listener's mind. Invoking sensory perceptions makes your story more engaging.

2. **Relatable Characters**: The characters in your story should reflect your target audience. They should exhibit both strengths and vulnerabilities that your audience can identify with.

3. **Emotional Connection**: Stories that evoke emotions, whether happiness, sadness, surprise, or anger, are likely to be more memorable.

4. **Suspense and Surprise**: Intrigue and unexpected twists will keep your audience on the edge of their seats and engage them till the end.

5. **Simplicity and Clarity**: The overall narrative should be so clear and straightforward that anyone listening to the story should easily understand it and recount it to someone else.

6.4. Implementing Storytelling in Your Business Strategy

After you've developed your business story, it is time to implement it strategically. This means integrating storytelling into all aspects of your business strategy including branding, marketing, leadership, and HR.

• In branding, storytelling defines who you are as a company, what sets you apart from your competitors, and why customers should care about your brand.

- In marketing, engaging narratives are used in creating ads, social media posts, or blog articles that influence consumer behavior.

- For leaders, stories can be used to motivate employees, articulate company vision, or explain the decision-making process.

- In HR, stories can be used to communicate company policy, instill company values, or narrate success stories.

By aligning storytelling with your business strategy, you can ensure seamless communication of your organizational values and objectives to your stakeholders.

6.5. Conclusion

Business storytelling is not a passing fad. It is an integral part of any organization that wants to build meaningful relationships and tangible value. Weaving a strategic narrative evolves brands from mere service or product providers to thought leaders with a clear vision and purpose. Eliciting authentic emotions and creating memorable moments, the right story can captivate your audience like no other tool. Invest in strategic storytelling, and let your narrative set the stage for your business success.

Chapter 7. Amplifying Brand Identity Through Storytelling

Storytelling is not a new invention; it stretches back to the dawn of humanity, serving as a fundamental tool for communication and understanding. Today we will delve into this age-old tactic and explore how it applies to a modern context—specifically, how it can amplify your brand identity. To begin, we must first understand brand identity and storytelling in sufficient depth.

7.1. Understanding Brand Identity

In the bustling marketplace, where numerous brands clamor for consumer attention, a powerful brand identity can make the difference between obscurity and recognition. Your brand identity is more than just a logo, a slogan, or a catchy jingle—it is the heart and soul of your company. It is the distinctive set of characteristics and values that possesses measurable influence over your customer's purchasing behavior.

Your brand identity informs how you want your business to be perceived, and so it shapes your tone of voice, visual assets, values, and overall customer experience. In developing your brand identity, you should consider which elements will genuinely resonate with your customers and differentiate your business from competitors.

7.2. Harnessing the Power of Storytelling

Now, consider storytelling—an intimate human experience that creates emotional bonds, fosters understanding, and propels people to action. Storytelling brings people together; it helps us find common ground and establish connections.

Even in the world of business, an artfully crafted narrative can make a significant impact. Weave an engaging story about your product, your company, or your customer, and watch as it engages emotions, facilitates understanding, establishes relevance, and encourages customer loyalty.

7.3. How Storytelling Enhances Brand Identity

Bringing together brand identity and storytelling can have transformative results. A narrative that reflects your brand's values, aspirations, and vision retains intellectual and emotional appeal for your audience. It helps your audience fully grasp who you are, what you offer, and what makes your brand unique.

When a brand can transform its values and mission into a compelling narrative, it can foster a profound sense of association in its customers. This association not only brings your brand to life and makes it more relatable, but it also amplifies your brand identity.

7.4. The Four Corners of Crafting a Brand Narrative

Building an enthralling brand narrative requires strategic thought, emotional intelligence, and a keen understanding of your audience's needs and wants.

1. Empathy: Understanding your customers, their pain points, their dreams, and their daily lives is paramount. The more you empathize, the more you can create narratives that resonate with them emotionally.

2. Authenticity: Today's consumers are adept at distinguishing genuine narratives from calculated marketing ploys. Remain honest and transparent, reflecting your real-world experiences and maintaining consistent messaging.

3. Inspiration: Your audience wants to be inspired; they want stories that uplift, motivate, and encourage. Therefore, focus on narratives that shed positive light on your brand.

4. Connection: Your audience should see themselves in your story. Achieve this through familiar contexts and scenarios, promoting inclusivity and relatability.

7.5. Case Study: Amplifying Brand Identity

Let's study a practical example: Nike. This globally recognized brand has skillfully interwoven its brand identity with compelling narratives. "Just Do It," their iconic slogan, captures their drive for individual achievement and resilience. Each marketing campaign tells a story grounded in determination, overcoming adversity, and individual greatness, echoing the brand's identity and values.

This storytelling approach has amplified Nike's brand identity, making it easier for customers to identify with them and their product offerings. The result is a dedicated customer base and strong brand loyalty.

7.6. Leveraging Storytelling for Your Brand

To leverage storytelling in amplifying your brand identity, start by understanding your target audience. Delve into their interests, expectations, values, and motivations. Sketch out your brand's personality traits and how they align with your customers. Then, construct stories around these traits and customer experiences.

Of course, storytelling in business is more than sharing anecdotes or entertaining tales. It is about weaving a narrative with strategic goals in mind—forming connections, arousing emotions, inspiring action, and driving growth. Striking visuals, unforgettable characters, and inspiring dialogue can serve your business concretely by reinforcing brand perceptions, fostering loyalty, and driving conversions.

Your brand story can unfold across various platforms, such as your website, social media channels, email campaigns, and marketing materials. Consistency is key in maintaining the integrity of your brand identity. Continually revisit your narrative and adjust as your brand evolves, ensuring it remains a genuine articulation of who you are as a brand and your distinct value.

In conclusion, when genuinely crafted, stories can be a potent tool in amplifying your brand identity, generating emotional engagement, and promoting brand loyalty among your audience. Together, brand identity and storytelling forge a powerful narrative that stands loud and clear in the noisy marketplace, guiding your business towards greater visibility, reach, and growth.

Chapter 8. Utilizing Storytelling in Leadership and Employee Engagement

Incorporating narratives into leadership is an art, one that has proven itself to be an effective vehicle for driving change and fostering growth. From the earliest cave drawings to modern-day viral videos, stories have always played a pivotal role in connecting people, evoking emotions, and influencing behaviors.

8.1. Leveraging the Power of Storytelling in Leadership

Effective leaders don't just dictate; they inspire. They motivate their teams not with data and charts, but by shaping a compelling narrative that resonates on a deeply human level. Stories capture the essence of the organization's purpose, giving each employee a reason to strive for more. When a leader shares a story that shines a light on the company's vision or mission, it melds individual efforts into a singular force focused on achieving that common goal.

Remember, the essence of leadership storytelling isn't the story itself, but the emotions, values, and visions it conveys. This emotional connection encourages employees to go above and beyond their call of duty, pushing the organization further towards its strategic objectives.

8.2. Crafting Your Leadership Narrative

The first step towards harnessing the power of storytelling in leadership is crafting your narrative. Leaders must understand their own story before they can share it with others. Ask yourself: why are you here? What do you believe in? What defining moments have shaped your leadership style? Reflecting on these questions will help craft a story that is uniquely yours - one that is genuine, memorable, and relatable.

Once you've established your own narrative, it's time to create a compelling story for your organization. This isn't about crafting a PR-friendly mission statement. Instead, it's about dig deeper, finding your organization's 'why', and communicating it in a way that connects with your team's core values and aspirations.

8.3. The Impact of Storytelling on Employee Engagement

A crucial yet often overlooked aspect of business operations is employee engagement. Engaged employees are motivated, productive, and more likely to stay with the company. Storytelling can play an essential role in fostering this engagement.

Why? Because facts tell, but stories sell. They sell visions, ideas, strategies, and even corporate culture. When employees are invested in the story, they're invested in the company. They feel like they're a part of something larger than themselves, boosting morale, productivity, and loyalty.

8.4. Building a Connection Through Stories

Perhaps the most unique aspect of storytelling is its power to build connections. Stories allow leaders to show their vulnerability, admit their mistakes, and share their victories. This authenticity builds trust and fosters an environment of openness.

When employees see their leaders as 'real' people, they are more likely to express their ideas, take risks, and contribute to the organization's growth. It encourages a culture of transparency, which in turns leads to higher engagement and, ultimately, stronger performance.

8.5. Implementing Storytelling for Strategic Growth

The driving force behind the effectiveness of storytelling lies in weaving it through all elements of leadership and strategic planning. Use stories to define problem statements, convey solutions, and explain strategic decisions. By doing so, you take complex business jargon and translate it into a language all your employees can understand.

Remember, people don't buy products; they buy stories. The same principle applies within organizations. Employees don't buy into strategies; they buy into the stories that define the strategy's purpose, relevance, and potential impact.

By harnessing the power of storytelling, you're not just leading; you're inspiring. You're not just engaging employees; you're empowering them. And in doing so, you're setting your organization on a path towards strategic growth and meaningful success.

In conclusion, storytelling is not an add-on to leadership or employee engagement but rather an integral part of it. By incorporating storytelling, leaders can forge stronger relations, build a more engaged workforce, and steer their organizations towards the strategic growth they aspire to achieve.

Chapter 9. Crisis Management: The Role of Storytelling

In the world of corporate crisis management, storytelling is a powerful tool for shaping perceptions, fostering engagement, and steering outcomes towards desired objectives. Its value lies in its ability to make complex issues accessible, relate abstract challenges to everyday experiences, and spur action through emotional resonance and personal relatability.

9.1. Understanding Crisis Management Through Storytelling

A crisis is defined by uncertainty, high stakes, and urgency. Stakeholders, including employees, consumers, investors, and the general public, are often anxious and in need of clear, reliable, and empathetic communication. Storytelling humanizes the faceless corporation, offering an accessible channel for providing necessary information, resolving confusion or misunderstanding, and articulating a path forward.

During a crisis, storytelling can be instrumental in its management by providing context and framing narratives. Through masterfully crafted narratives, you can influence how your stakeholders perceive and interpret the situation, driving reactions, opinions, and decisions.

9.2. Using Storytelling to Craft a Crisis Response

To leverage the power of storytelling in crisis management, you need a strategic and thoughtful approach. The following steps provide a scalable framework:

1. Identify the Core Conflict: Every good story revolves around a conflict. In crisis management, the conflict comprises the problem the company is facing. Be concrete and forthright about this.

2. Articulate the Challenge: In every crisis, there is a challenge to be overcome. This challenge must be starkly presented, showing your audience the necessity and urgency of overcoming it.

3. Draw a Path Toward Resolution: A story without a satisfying resolution leaves an audience uneasy. In the context of storytelling for crisis management, the resolution is the action plan to overcome the conflict.

4. Emphasize the Lessons Learned: The resolution should end with the company learning from the crisis and taking steps to prevent a recurrence. This demonstrates adaptability and resilience.

9.3. Case Study: Company ABC and Crisis Management

Consider a case study where Company ABC was accused of unsustainable manufacturing practices. The accusation triggered a media uproar, and the company needed to act swiftly to manage the crisis.

1. Core Conflict: The company acknowledged the accusations, explaining that some of its products were using less environmentally friendly processes. They didn't shy away from

accepting responsibility.

2. Articulating the Challenge: The challenge was to bring their processes in line with sustainable practices. The company recognized that its customers cared deeply about sustainability, and that the accusations challenged their trustworthy relations.

3. Drawing a Path Toward Resolution: The company developed a comprehensive action plan to overhaul its manufacturing processes by investing in renewable resources.

4. Emphasizing Lessons Learned: The conclusion of their narrative focused on company ABC's new commitment to sustainability, their investment in green technology and their dedication towards full transparency in future operations.

9.4. Common Mistakes When Using Storytelling for Crisis Management

Narratives are potent, but if misused, they can backfire. Avoid spin, minimize jargon and technical language, ensure that different corporate messages do not contradict each other, and avoid blaming others. Furthermore, respond to your critics in a professional manner.

In conclusion, a well-crafted story can be an invaluable strategy in crisis management. By being proactive, taking responsibility and explaining the steps your company is taking to mitigate the situation, you can control your brand's narrative. This will result in earned respect from your stakeholders, establish trust, and create a bridge towards future communication and cooperation. The art of storytelling is the ultimate exercise in empathy, understanding, and connection with your audience. Your stories will define how others perceive your resolution of the crisis, establishing a foundation for all future interactions.

Chapter 10. Digital Storytelling: Integrating Technology and Narrative

Part of the sublime power of storytelling in business is its timeless nature, enhanced, not replaced, by advancements in technology. In this digital age, the traditional foundations of storytelling persist as ever, albeit with a modern twist. Nowhere else does this intersection of age-old storytelling techniques and digital advances reveal itself more impressively than in the practice of digital storytelling.

10.1. Understanding Digital Storytelling

Digital storytelling refers to the utilization of digital tools and platforms to craft and disseminate narratives. It's about leveraging modern technological strengths to significantly boost the efficacy of your storytelling. In essence, it is not just about the content of the narrative presented, but how you present it.

These narratives can take various forms, including audio recordings, videos, blog posts, podcasts, slideshow presentations, or interactive infographics. They all have the potential to encourage consumer engagement, increase brand awareness, and drive growth.

10.2. The Importance of Digital Storytelling in Business

As the digital landscape intensifies, businesses worldwide race to improve their online presence. Digital storytelling comes forward as a strategic approach to make unique brand identities resound through the clutter.

A digital narrative allows a business to tell its story in a more engaging, interactive, and comprehensive way. This contributes to building better customer relationships, fostering loyalty, and eventually leading to sales conversion and business growth.

10.3. Effective Elements of Digital Storytelling

Digital storytelling is as varied as the businesses that use it, but there are recurring elements that can drive its effectiveness.

Table 1. +Caption: Elements of Digital Storytelling.

Element	Description	Examples
Multimedia	Utilization of images, sound, videos, and text to enhance the storytelling experience.	Podcasts where the host narrates a brand's story, mixed with relevant image presentation.
Interaction	This refers to allowing consumers to engage with the story	Interactive infographics.
Personalization	Using data analytics to tailor content to specific user preferences and behavior	AI-driven personalized email campaigns.

These elements aren't strictly separate. In fact, in most powerful digital stories, these criteria overlap and enhance each other.

10.4. Developing a Compelling Digital Story

Creating a compelling digital story requires keen attention to content, structure, and presentation, but remember that at the core of any story is its human element.

Begin by identifying what you want your story to achieve: cast a vision, establish your business' values, or showcase your products. Then, weave this goal subtly into a narrative that revolves around people, whether they be your customers, employees, or society at large. Remember to maintain authenticity throughout the narrative as a recognizable human touch is an invaluable ingredient of any successful story.

Use multimedia elements wisely to enhance the narrative — a well-placed image, video, or sound clip can amplify the effects of the story. However, the misuse of multimedia can easily overwhelm and disengage your audience. Strive for a balance, always favoring quality over quantity.

Finally, don't forget to provide opportunities for interaction within the narrative, whether through clickable links, feedback sections, quizzes, or other interactive tools. This allows the audience to be part of the story, increasing engagement and maximizing the impact of your narrative.

10.5. Implementing Digital Storytelling: Challenges and Solutions

Challenges accompany any business venture, and digital storytelling isn't an exception. However, they provide opportunities for learning, growth, and improvement. Some commonly encountered challenges include:

- Ensuring the story aligns with the brand and communicates its purpose effectively.
- Choosing the right digital platform for the story.
- Creating an engaging, clear, and compelling narrative.
- Maximizing reach to the intended audience.
- Monitoring the effectiveness of the story.

To overcome these challenges, consider the following solutions:

- Develop a clear brand narrative before embarking on digital storytelling.
- Conduct thorough research to determine the platform preference of your targeted audience.
- Leverage data analytics to tailor storytelling strategies in line with audience preferences.
- Regularly assess and adjust your storytelling strategies based on audience responses and feedback.

10.6. Digital Storytelling: The Future

The future of digital storytelling holds endless possibilities, with emerging technologies such as virtual reality (VR), augmented reality

(AR), and artificial intelligence (AI) pushing the boundaries of what can be achieved. Imagine a story that transcends auditory and visual perceptions, stepping into a world where users can interact with narratives in a 3D virtual world.

The marriage of technology and narrative in digital storytelling offers individuals, brands, and organizations the unique chance to connect with their audiences at a much deeper level. As digital technologies continue to evolve, so will the capacity for businesses to tell their stories in increasingly engaging, interactive, and personalized ways.

Indeed, mastering digital storytelling is not just about staying ahead in the digital business revolution; it is about crafting narratives that will resonate, inspire, and endure. It is about drawing audiences into the heart of your brand and business, and there, strengthening the bonds of connection, trust, interaction, and mutual growth. It is storytelling — redefined by the digital age.

Chapter 11. Case Studies: Successful Business Storytelling Examples

=== The Power of Apple's 'Think Different' Campaign

One example of a successful business storytelling campaign is Apple's 'Think Different'. Launched in 1997, the campaign features black and white pictures of iconic personalities such as Albert Einstein, Bob Dylan, and Martin Luther King Jr. This campaign was Apple's attempt to promote its values rather than its products, a bold move that paid off.

The story was about uniqueness and innovation - a message that resonates with the Apple brand. Their message underscored the paradox of thinking differently - it may feel uncomfortable, but it is also the only way to effect real change. This narrative has stuck with the brand, giving it a modern, innovative, and unique image.

This kind of emotional connection with customers is what storytelling in business is all about. Apple's 'Think Different' campaign connects emotionally, inspiring consumers to be individual and innovative like the personalities in their advertisements. They were not selling just a product; they sold a lifestyle, a mentality, and a culture.

=== The Power of Nike's 'Just Do It' Slogan

Another compelling business story comes from Nike with their famous 'Just Do It' slogan. It's a perfect example of a narrative that tells a story in just three words. The statement encapsulates the spirit of determination, perseverance, and grit, attributes closely associated with sports and athletes.

Launched in 1988, the campaign was based on a simple but powerful idea - inspiring people to overcome procrastination and chase their dreams. Over the years, this slogan has become more than a marketing tool; it has become a rallying cry for people to push their limits and achieve their goals. It represents the emotional journey of every sportsperson - reluctance, determination, exertion, struggle, and ultimately, achievement.

Through their 'Just Do It' campaign, Nike has continuously propelled the empowering narrative of sportsmen. It's a narrative that connects with customers, making them feel a part of the journey. As a result, they are not just buying sports wear; they are buying into a story of tenacity and achievement.

=== Warby Parker and the Quest to Revolutionize Eyewear

Warby Parker presents another case study of successful business storytelling. The company's narrative is rooted in the quest to provide stylish, high-quality, and affordable eyewear, a niche they identified in the market.

The company's name is inspired by two characters from Jack Kerouac's journals: Warby Pepper and Zagg Parker, instilling a sense of literature and history in the brand. But the story doesn't stop there: Warby Parker also presented itself as a David against Goliath, a small company intent on challenging the traditional, and expensive, eyewear market dominated by a few giants.

However, the most compelling part of Warby Parker's narrative is their Buy a Pair, Give a Pair program. For each pair of glasses sold, another pair is contributed to someone in need. Customers are directly involved in a heartening narrative of giving back and are thus buying not just eyewear, but also contributing to a cause.

=== Tesla: Driving towards a Sustainable Future

Tesla's narrative revolves around innovative technology and

sustainable energy. Elon Musk, the CEO of Tesla Motors, uses storytelling very effectively to create a vision of a future where sustainable technology is paramount.

Musk's vision of changing the auto industry by creating electric vehicles and transforming how we perceive sustainability sews the narrative together. His audacious goal of colonizing Mars further adds an unusual and intriguing layer to Tesla's story. This narrative captures imagination and rallies supporters, investors and customers alike.

Tesla isn't merely selling cars; they are selling a vision of the future. This narrative strategy is very effective because it appeals to people's hopes and aspirations. It is the perfect example of how business storytelling can help in branding and positioning your products.

=== Conclusion: The Transformative Power of Storytelling in Business

These case studies show that connecting to customers on an emotional level through storytelling can be an incredibly powerful tool. From Apple's audacity to Nike's empowering spirit, Warby Parker's empathy to Tesla's visionary idea, storytelling has proven to be a key component in their successes.

Each of these companies sells products. But more importantly, they sell stories. They have realized that customers don't just buy products; they buy into narratives that connect with their emotions and aspirations. In essence, successful business storytelling transforms customers from mere consumers into brand ambassadors. It creates a deeper bond that cannot be solely measured in balance sheets.

In analyzing these examples, we hope that you can identify potential narratives within your business and leverage them to develop meaningful connections with your customers and stakeholders. Start thinking about how you can package your corporate narrative and embed it into your marketing, advertising, and public relations. Turn your story into your advantage, and see how it can drive your strategic growth.